Math Around Us

# Sorting at the Market

Tracey Steffora

Heinemann Library
Chicago, Illinois

**www.capstonepub.com**
Visit our website to find out
more information about
Heinemann-Raintree books.

**To order:**

☎ Phone 800-747-4992

💻 Visit www.capstonepub.com
to browse our catalog and order online.

Edited by Rebecca Rissman, Tracey Steffora, and Catherine Veitch
Designed by Joanna Hinton-Malivoire
Picture research by Elizabeth Alexander
Production by Victoria Fitzgerald
Originated by Capstone Global Library Ltd

**Acknowledgments**
The author and publisher are grateful to the following for
permission to reproduce photographs: Alamy: blickwinkel, 14, DC
Premiumstock, 17, ephotocorp, 21, 23 bottom, imageBROKER,
10, Wiskerke, 18; Capstone Studio: Karon Dubke, 11, 12, 15,
16, 19, 20; Getty Images Inc.: Brigitte Sporrer, 7; iStockphoto:
Stephanie DeLay, 9, 23 top; Shutterstock: Andre Nantel, Back
Cover, 13, hpf, 5, Manuel Fernandes, Cover, 8, Sia Chen How, 22,
Tupungato, 4

We would like to thank Nancy Harris, Dee Reid, and Diana Bentley
for their assistance in the preparation of this book.

Every effort has been made to contact copyright holders of
material reproduced in this book. Any omissions will be rectified in
subsequent printings if notice is given to the publisher.

**Library of Congress Cataloging-in-Publication Data**
Steffora, Tracey.
   Sorting at the market / Tracey Steffora.
      p. cm.—(Math around us)
   Includes bibliographical references and index.
   ISBN 978-1-4329-4927-3 (hc)—ISBN 978-1-4329-4935-8
(pb) 1. Set theory—Juvenile literature. I. Title.
   QA248.S773 2011
   511.3'22—dc22                    2010030771

# Contents

# At the Market

We sort things every day.

There are many ways we sort things at the market.

## Shopping List

| vegetables | fruits |
|---|---|
| potatoes | bananas |
| beets | strawberries |
| green beans | grapes |

We sort things on a list.

We sort things in bags.

We sort things in baskets.

recycle

trash

We sort things in bins.

# Color

We sort things by color.

How would you sort these peppers?

Some are yellow. Some are green.
Some are red.

These flowers are sorted by color.

# Size

We sort things by size.

How would you sort these tomatoes?

Some are big. Some are small.

These hats are sorted by size.

# Shape

We sort things by shape.

How would you sort this bread?

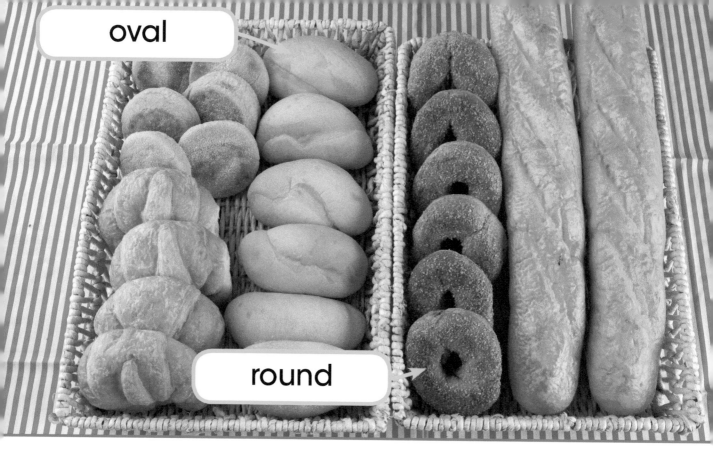

oval

round

Some are round. Some are ovals.
Some are long and thin.

These lanterns are sorted by shape.

# Sorting All Around

There are things to sort everywhere!
How can you sort things?

# Picture Glossary

 **bin** a container that holds trash or recycling

 **lantern** a type of light

# Index

**Notes to Parents and Teachers**

**Before reading**

Being able to classify and group items into a set is an important mathematical concept for children to acquire. Prepare a selection of circles, squares, and triangles of various colors and have each child choose one out of a bowl. Ask all children holding triangles to stand in one group, all those holding squares in another group, and all those holding circles in a third group. Explain that the objects have just been sorted by shape. Have all the children come back together and ask them to get into groups by color. Explain that when we sort objects, we are finding something that is alike about them and putting them in groups.

**After reading**

Extend children's understanding of fruits and vegetables by explaining that fruits are the part of the plant that contains seeds, and vegetables are other plant parts that we eat (e.g. roots, leaves, stems). With children, review the list on page 6 and discuss other fruits and vegetables that can be added to each category of the list. If possible, provide actual examples or photos of the items. You might even have children sort the objects further (green vegetables, orange vegetables, red fruits, etc.).